Reading STREET

Grade 1

Scott Foresman

Phonics and Spelling Practice Book

PEARSON
Scott Foresman

Editorial Offices: Glenview, Illinois • Parsippany, New Jersey • New York, New York
Sales Offices: Boston, Massachusetts • Duluth, Georgia • Glenview, Illinois
Coppell, Texas • Sacramento, California • Mesa, Arizona

ISBN: 0-328-14646-3

25 26 ·V011 - 16 15 14 13

Contents

Unit 3 Changes

Unit 4 Treasures

Unit 5 Great Ideas

Steps for Spelling New Words

Here is a plan to use when you study your spelling words.

Step 1
Look at the word. **Say** it and listen to the sounds.

Step 2
Spell the word aloud.

Step 3
Think about the spelling. Is there anything special to remember?

Step 4
Picture the word with your eyes shut.

Step 5
Look at the word and **write** it.

Step 6
Cover the word. Picture it and **write** it again. **Check** its spelling. Did you get it right?

There are 6 steps to remember. Use this plan a few times. You will see how it can help you.

 Jack wants to learn the new spelling word *bump*. In Step 1, he looks at the word, says it, and listens to all the sounds.

 In Step 2, he spells the word aloud.

 In Step 3, he thinks about how the word is spelled.

 In Step 4, Jack sees the word with his eyes shut.

 In Step 5, Jack looks at the word and he writes it on paper at the same time.

 Finally, in Step 6, Jack covers the word. He pictures what it looks like. Then he writes it again. He checks to see if it is correct.

Rhyming Helpers

If you can match a new list word to a word you know with the same spelling at the end, you will have two words that rhyme. Then the old word can be a helper for the new word. These words are Rhyming Helpers.

I can spell <u>train</u> because I know how to spell <u>rain</u>.

Rain is the rhyming helper for *train*. *Train* and *rain* rhyme and they have the same ending.

I can spell <u>beach</u> because I know how to spell <u>each</u>.

Each is the rhyming helper for *beach*. They rhyme and have the same ending.

Look at your new spelling word. Think of a word that rhymes. Be sure it ends the same. This word can be your rhyming helper.

Here is another example of a rhyming helper.

What rhyming helper will help me spell <u>treat</u>?

How about <u>eat</u>? It rhymes. It is spelled the same at the end.

I can spell <u>treat</u> because I know how to spell <u>eat</u>.

Eat is Beth's rhyming helper for *treat*.

Watch out! Some words rhyme but have different spellings. The word *feet* sounds like *treat*, but the rhyming sound is spelled in a different way.

Treat ends in **e-a-t**, *feet* ends in **e-e-t**. *Feet* is not a rhyming helper for *treat*.

Here are more Rhyming Helpers.

Old spelling word	New spelling word
d**own**	fr**own**
out	sh**out**

Problem Parts

Everybody has words that are hard to spell. Sometimes the problem is with a few letters. This is a good time to use the **Problem Parts** strategy.

One of the words you will learn to spell is *fur*.

The **f** in *fur* is easy. The rest of the word is hard. Here are steps to follow in the Problem Parts strategy.

Step 1
Ask yourself which part of the word is giving you a problem.

Step 2
Write the word and underline the problem part.

Step 3
Picture the word. Think about the problem part. What does it look like?

Picture your word and see the problem part. Then spell your word.

Here is another example of using the Problem Part strategy.
The word you want to learn is *pillow*.
Think about the word.

Step 1
Ask yourself which part of the word
is the problem part.

Step 2
Write the word. Underline the two *l*'s.

Step 3
Picture the word.
Think hard about what the problem part
looks like. Picture the problem part in
very large letters. That can help you
remember the problem part.

Remember, sometimes only part of a word is hard.
Maybe just a few letters are tricky. If you learn the
problem part, you can spell the whole word!

Frequently Misspelled Words!

The words below are words that are misspelled the most by students your age. Pay special attention to these frequently misspelled words as you read, write, and spell.

because	with	were
when	have	people
like	very	about
they	friend	play
went	my	what
too	was	our
said	would	their
there	are	nice
house	want	of
know	friends	once

© Pearson Education

Words with Short *a*

Look at the word. **Say** it. **Listen** for the short *a* sound.

Write each word.	**Check** it.

1. at

2. can

3. cat

4. back

5. dad

6. am

7. bat

8. mad

9. ran

10. sack

Look at the word. **Say** it. **Write** the word.

11. way _____ 12. on _____

School + Home

Home Activity Your child is learning to spell words with the short *a* vowel sound. To practice at home, have your child point to the short *a* vowel sound, pronounce the word and write it.

Words with Short *a*

Write two list words that rhyme with **pan**.

1. __c_____

2. __r_____

Write two list words that rhyme with **sad**.

3. __m_____

4. __d_____

Write two list words that rhyme with **tack**.

5. __b_____

6. __s_____

Write two list words that rhyme with **hat**.

7. __c_____

8. __b_____

Write the missing words.

am   at

9. Look _____ me.   10. I _____ on a box.

Spelling Words
at
can
cat
back
dad
am
bat
mad
ran
sack

School + Home

Home Activity Your child wrote words with the short *a* vowel sound. Point to a picture on this page and have your child spell the word.

© Pearson Education

Words with Short *a*

Find a list word to finish the sentence.
Write it on the line.

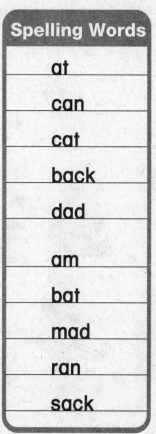

Spelling Words

at
can
cat
back
dad
am
bat
mad
ran
sack

1. The bug _____ hop.

2. I _____ sad.

3. His _____ has a van.

4. The dog _____ .

5. I _____ the ball.

6. Look _____ the fox.

7. I fed my _____ .

8. Put the can in the _____ .

9. He is _____ at me.

10. Go _____ to bed.

Home Activity Your child wrote spelling words to complete sentences. Help your child make up a new sentence for each spelling word.

Words with Short *a*

Circle the word that names the picture.

Spelling Words

at
can
cat
back
dad
am
bat
mad
ran
sack

1.
sack
can
cat

2.
cat
bat
dad

3.
back
sack
bat

4.
dad
ran
mad

5.
can
bat
ran

6.
can
ran
cat

Say the words. Circle the two words that are the same.
Write the word.

_____

7. can   at   at   am   7. _____

8. back   sack   at   back   8. _____

9. ran   am   can   am   9. _____

10. ran   mad   mad   dad   10. _____

School + Home

Home Activity Your child has been learing to spell words with short *a*. To review what your child has learned, take turns thinking of and spelling simple words with short *a*.

4 Unit 1 Week 1 **Day 4**   **Spelling Practice Book**

© Pearson Education

Words with Short *i*

Look at the word. **Say** it. **Listen** for the short *i* sound.

Write the word.	**Check** it.

1. in

2. it

3. did

4. sit

5. six

6. fix

7. lip

8. mix

9. pin

10. wig

High-Frequency Words

11. and

12. take

© Pearson Education

School + Home **Home Activity** Your child is learning to spell words with the short *i* vowel sound. To practice at home, have your child pronounce each word and spell it out loud.

Name _____

Words with Short *i*

Write letters to finish the word.

1. **p** _____

2. **s** _____

3. **w** _____

4. **l** _____

5. **s** _____

6. **m** _____

7. **f** _____

8. **i** _____

Write the missing words.

it   did

9. I hit _____ .

10. Yes, I _____ .

Home Activity Your child spelled words with the short *i* vowel sound. Point to a picture on this page and have your child spell the word.

6 Unit 1 Week 2 **Day 2**

Spelling Practice Book

© Pearson Education

Words with Short *i*

Spelling Words				
in	it	did	sit	six
fix	lip	mix	pin	wig

Circle a word to finish the sentence. **Write** the word.

1. He is   **fix   six   pin** .   _____

2. I bit my   **lip   did   sit** .   _____

3. Put   **sit   it   fix**   in the box.   _____

4. Can she   **in   wig   fix**   it?   _____

5. You can   **sit   lip   six**   here.   _____

6. His   **did   wig   in**   is red.   _____

7. They   **pin   six   did**   not go.   _____

8. Help me find a   **pin   sit   in** .   _____

9. I will   **it   six   mix**   red and blue.   _____

10. Look   **sit   in   lip**   the mug.   _____

Home Activity Your child wrote spelling words to complete sentences. Read a sentence, say the spelling word, and ask your child to spell the word. Continue with other sentences.

Words with Short *i*

Write the missing letters. Then write the words.

1. ☐ **t**   ------------------
   _____

2. **f** ☐ ☐   ------------------
   _____

3. ☐ **n** ☐   ------------------
   _____

4. **s** ☐ **x**   ------------------
   _____

Spelling Words
in
it
did
sit
six
fix
lip
mix
pin
wig

Write a list word that rhymes with each word.

5. pig
_____

_____

6. hip
_____

_____

7. lid
_____
----

8. tin
_____
----

9. fit
_____
----

10. six
_____

Home Activity Your child has been learning to spell words with short *i*. To review, draw some circles. Have your child write a short-*i* word in each circle.

Spelling Practice Book

Words with Short *o*

Look at the word. **Say** it. **Listen** for the short *o* sound.

Write the word.	**Check** it.

1. mom
2. hot
3. hop
4. pot
5. pop
6. ox
7. lock
8. mop
9. got
10. rock

High-Frequency Words

11. help   12. use

School + Home   **Home Activity** Your child is learning to spell words with a short *o* vowel sound. Have your child write each word and point to the short *o* vowel sound.

Words with Short *o*

Spelling Words				
mom	hot	hop	pot	pop
ox	lock	mop	got	rock

Write a word that rhymes.

1. **sock** on a

_____

_____

2. **hot**

_____

_____

3. **box** on an

_____

_____

4. **block** on a

_____

_____

5. **top**

_____

_____

6. **Tom** and

_____

_____

Draw a line from the word to its shape.
Write the word in the shape.

hot

mop

pop

got

7.

8.

9.

10.

Home Activity Your child spelled words with the short *o* vowel sound. Help your child spell each word and then think of a rhyming word.

© Pearson Education

Words with Short *o*

Find a list word to finish the sentence.
Write it on the line.

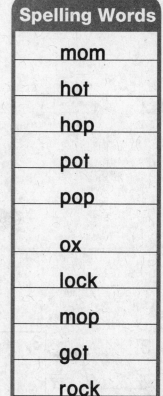

Spelling Words

mom
hot
hop
pot
pop
ox
lock
mop
got
rock

_____
----
1. Fill the _____ .

_____
----
2. She is my _____ .

_____
----
3. I will _____ up the mess.

_____
----
4. Frogs can _____ .

_____
----
5. The sun is _____ .

_____
----
6. He is my _____ .

_____
----
7. Put a _____ on his van.

_____
----
8. I _____ wet.

_____
----
9. Will an _____ pull the cart?

_____
----
10. The _____ is big.

School + Home

Home Activity Your child wrote spelling words to complete sentences. Have your child make up and write new sentences for several of the words.

Words with Short *o*

Write the words in the puzzle.

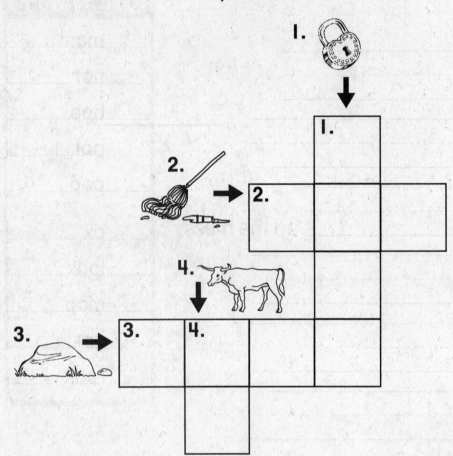

Spelling Words
mom
hot
hop
pot
pop
ox
lock
mop
got
rock

Connect the matching hearts.

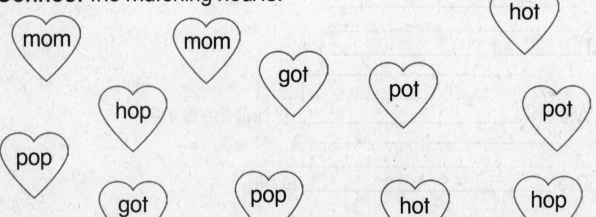

Home Activity Your child has been learning to spell words with short *o*. Have your child think of and write words that rhyme with *spot* or *stop*.

Spelling Practice Book

Adding -s

Look at the word. **Say** it. **Think:** Does the word end in *s*?

Write the word.	**Check** it.
1. nap	
2. naps	
3. sit	
4. sits	
5. win	
6. wins	
7. fit	
8. fits	
9. hit	
10. hits	

High-Frequency Words

11. her   12. too

Home Activity Your child is learning to spell words that end in *s*. To practice at home, have your child say each word aloud. Next help your child create a sentence using each word.

Name _____

Adding -s

Write list words to finish the sentences.

Spelling Words
nap
naps
sit
sits
win
wins
fit
fits
hit
hits

1. They _____ .

2. It _____ .

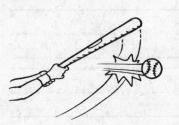

3. They _____ .

4. He _____ .

5. They _____ in bed.

6. He _____ in bed.

7. They _____ on mats.

8. He _____ on a mat.

9. They _____ the race.

10. He _____ the race.

Home Activity Your child spelled pairs of words with and without the *s* ending. Point to a word on this page and have your child spell the other word in the pair.

14 Unit 1 Week 4 **Day 2**   **Spelling Practice Book**

Adding -s

Write list words to finish the sentences.

Spelling Words
nap
naps
sit
sits
win
wins
fit
fits
hit
hits

1. The pups _____ .

2. The pup _____ .

3. The pups _____ .

4. The pup _____ .

5. I can _____ the game.

6. She _____ all the games.

7. The wind _____ the flag.

8. He can _____ the ball.

9. Will the hat _____ in the box?

10. My mitt _____ you.

School + Home **Home Activity** Your child wrote spelling words to complete sentences. Have your child circle the list words that end in s.

© Pearson Education

Name _____

Adding -s

Draw a line to help Kit find her mitt.
Follow the words that rhyme with **Kit**.
Circle the words. **Write** the words.

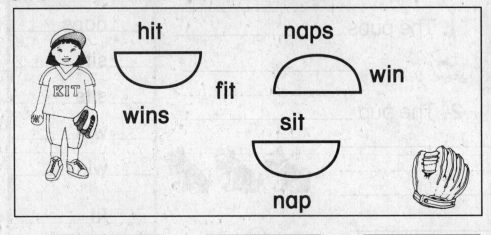

Spelling Words

nap
naps
sit
sits
win
wins
fit
fits
hit
hits

1. _____   2. _____   3. _____

Write these words in ABC order.

nap   wins   sits

4. _____   5. _____   6. _____

Write these words in ABC order.

win   hits   naps   fits

7. _____   8. _____

9. _____   10. _____

School + Home

Home Activity Your child has been learning to spell words that end in *s*. Help your child look on food boxes and cans for words that end in *s*.

Words with Short e

Look at the word. **Say** it. **Listen** for the short *e* sound.

Write the word.	**Check** it.

1. bed

2. men

3. red

4. step

5. ten

6. net

7. leg

8. jet

9. sled

10. wet

High-Frequency Words

11. saw

12. your

Home Activity Your child is learning to spell words with the short *e* vowel sound. To practice at home, have your child write each word and spell it out loud. Your child can then close his or her eyes and spell it again.

Words with Short *e*

Spelling Words				
bed	men	red	step	ten
net	leg	jet	sled	wet

Write three list words that rhyme with **pet**.

1. _____ 2. _____ 3. _____

Write three list words that rhyme with **Ted**.

4. _____ 5. _____ 6. _____

Write the missing word.

7. Let's make two _____ out of snow.

8. We need _____ buttons.

9. Do not _____ on his hat.

10. Does he need a _____ ?

leg
step
men
ten

© Pearson Education

School + Home

Home Activity Your child spelled words with the short e vowel sound. Have your child draw and label some of the words.

Words with Short e

Spelling Words
bed   men   red   step   ten   net   leg   jet   sled   wet

Choose a word to finish the sentence.
Fill in the circle. **Write** the word.

1. I made the ○ **bed** ○ **men** ○ **leg** . _____

2. Do not get me ○ **step** ○ **wet** ○ **net** ! _____

3. Her sock was ○ **sled** ○ **jet** ○ **red** . _____

4. Kick with your ○ **ten** ○ **net** ○ **leg** . _____

5. Kim has a ○ **red** ○ **sled** ○ **wet** . _____

6. A fish is in the ○ **net** ○ **ten** ○ **step** . _____

7. Sit on the ○ **ten** ○ **step** ○ **red** . _____

8. I will count to ○ **ten** ○ **jet** ○ **sled** . _____

9. We helped the ○ **wet** ○ **red** ○ **men** . _____

10. Did you ride on a ○ **jet** ○ **men** ○ **red** ? _____

Home Activity Your child wrote spelling words to complete sentences. Help your child find other spelling words that make sense in the sentences. For example, Sentence 1 could read "I made the **net**."

Words with Short e

Write the words.

1. _____

2. _____

3. _____

4. _____

Spelling Words
bed
men
red
step
ten
net
leg
jet
sled
wet

Circle the word that matches. **Write** it.

5. **bed**   bed   red

6. **men**   wet   men

7. **ten**   net   ten

8. **sled**   step   sled

9. **red**   red   sled

10. **wet**   net   wet

_____

_____

_____

_____

_____

_____

School + Home

Home Activity Your child has been learning to spell words with short e. Have your child think of and write words that rhyme with *set* or *fed*.

Spelling Practice Book

© Pearson Education

Name _____

Words with Short *u*

Look at the word. **Say** it. **Listen** for the short *u* sound.

Write the word.	**Check** it.
1. run		
2. cut		
3. must		
4. sun		
5. up		
6. bump		
7. jump		
8. bus		
9. nut		
10. rug		

High-Frequency Words

11. many _____ 12. into _____

School + Home **Home Activity** Your child is learning to spell words with the short *u* vowel sound. Practice at home by having your child write each word and circle the *u* in each word.

© Pearson Education

Words with Short *u*

Spelling Words				
run	cut	must	sun	up
bump	jump	bus	nut	rug

Write a list word to name the picture.

1. _____

2. _____

3. _____

4. _____

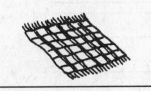

5. _____

6. _____

Read the clue. **Write** the list word.

7. It starts with **m**. It rhymes with **just**.

8. It starts with **u**. It rhymes with **cup**.

9. It starts with **c**. It rhymes with **hut**.

10. It starts with **b**. It rhymes with **pump**.

_____
_____
_____
_____
_____
_____

Home Activity Your child wrote words with the short *u* vowel sound. Take turns with your child making up clues and then guessing and spelling the word.

Words with Short *u*

Spelling Words				
run	cut	must	sun	up
bump	jump	bus	nut	rug

Write a list word to name the picture.

1. I wake _____ .

2. My feet hit the _____ .

3. I _____ go fast.

4. I _____ down the hall.

5. I _____ up an egg.

6. Mom eats a _____ .

7. We go in the _____ .

8. I _____ into the car.

9. The car hits a _____ .

10. We will go to the _____ .

Home Activity Your child wrote spelling words to complete a story. Help your child use some of the words in a story about his or her day.

© Pearson Education

Words with Short *u*

Write the words in the puzzle.

Spelling Words
run
cut
must
sun
up
bump
jump
bus
nut
rug

3.

2.

5.

4.

1.

Write the missing words.

cut run up must nut

6. Is it a _____ ?

7. I _____ get it.

8. I will go _____ .

9. We _____ fast.

10. You can _____ it.

Home Activity Your child has been learning to spell words with short *u*. Help your child find words with short *u* in library books or schoolbooks.

Words with *sh* or *th*

Look at the word. **Say** it. **Listen** for the *sh* or *th* sound.

Write the word.	**Check** it.
1. ship	
2. fish	
3. then	
4. shut	
5. with	
6. rush	
7. shell	
8. shop	
9. trash	
10. thin	

High-Frequency Words

11. want _____   12. good _____

School + Home

Home Activity Your child is learning to spell words with *sh* and *th*. To practice at home, say each word and have your child tell you if he or she is hearing the *sh* or *th* sound in each word.

Name _____

Words with *sh* or *th*

Spelling Words				
ship	fish	then	shut	with
rush	shell	shop	trash	thin

Find a list word to name the picture. **Write** it.

1. _____

2. _____

3. _____

4. _____

5. _____

6. _____

Unscramble the word. **Write** the word.

s	h	u	r

7. _____

i	t	h	w

8. _____

n	e	t	h

9. _____

n	t	h	i

10. _____

School + Home

Home Activity Your child wrote words with the *sh* or *th* sound. Say a list word. Ask if it has *sh* or *th*. Have your child spell the word.

26 Unit 2 Week 1 **Day 2**

Spelling Practice Book

© Pearson Education

Words with *sh* or *th*

Find a list word to finish the sentence.
Write it on the line.

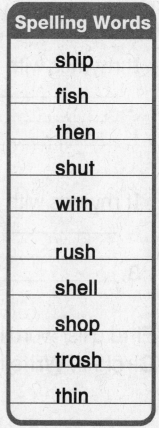

Spelling Words
ship
fish
then
shut
with
rush
shell
shop
trash
thin

_____

----

1. I will _____ home.

_____

----

2. Will you feed my _____ ?

_____

----

3. Come _____ me.

_____

----

4. Dad will be back _____ .

_____

----

5. Put the paper in the _____ can.

_____

----

6. This egg has a brown _____ .

_____

----

7. Do not _____ the door.

_____

----

8. We will _____ for a new cap.

_____

----

9. She came on a _____ .

_____

----

10. That dog is _____ .

Home Activity Your child wrote spelling words to complete sentences. Ask your child to write a sentence using two or more of the spelling words.

Name _____

Words with *sh* or *th*

Read the clue. **Write** a list word.

It rhymes with

_____

1. _____

It rhymes with

_____

2. _____

It rhymes with

_____

3. _____

It rhymes with

_____

4. _____

Spelling Words

Spelling Words
ship
fish
then
shut
with
rush
shell
shop
trash
thin

Find a list word in each row of letters.
Circle it. **Write** it.

r u s h t e   5. _____

t s h u t r   6. _____

s h o p t h   7. _____

s t r a s h   8. _____

w i f i s h   9. _____

r w i t h s   10. _____

fish
shut
trash
rush
shop
with

 Home Activity Your child has been learning to spell words with *sh* and *th*. Have your child circle *sh* and *th* in the spelling words.

© Pearson Education

Name _____

Words with Long *a*

Look at the word. **Say** it. **Listen** for the long *a* sound.

Write the word.	**Check** it.

1. face

2. made

3. age

4. safe

5. take

6. make

7. cage

8. cake

9. late

10. name

High-Frequency Words

11. could

12. old

School + Home

Home Activity Your child is learning to spell words with the long *a* sound. To practice at home, have your child say the word and spell it with eyes closed.

© Pearson Education

Words with Long *a*

Spelling Words

face	made	age	safe	take
make	cage	cake	late	name

Write three list words that rhyme with **rake**.

1. _____ 2. _____ 3. _____

Write two list words that rhyme with **page**.

4. _____ 5. _____

Write the missing word.

safe	face	name	late	made

6. Her _____ is Bo.

7. Bo _____ a dog.

8. Her _____ is happy.

9. Is that ball _____ ?

10. Can we stay _____ ?

 Home Activity Your child wrote words with the long *a* sound. Help your child think of words that rhyme with the spelling words.

Words with Long *a*

Spelling Words				
face	made	age	safe	take
make	cage	cake	late	name

Circle a word to finish the sentence. **Write** the word.

_____

1. I love   **cake   late   make**!   _____

2. Have a   **face   safe   name**   trip.   _____

3. I   **made   age   cake**   it.   _____

4. What is your   **made   late   name**?   _____

5. His   **age   face   make**   got red.   _____

6. What is in the   **cage   age   face**?   _____

7. She won't tell her   **cake   late   age**.   _____

8. Let's   **safe   made   make**   a kite.   _____

9. I like to stay up   **late   take   face**.   _____

10. We can   **age   take   cake**   turns.   _____

Home Activity Your child used spelling words to complete sentences. Have your child identify and write as many spelling words as possible to finish this sentence: *This is my_____*.

Words with Long *a*

© Pearson Education

Spelling Words

face	made	age	safe	take
make	cage	cake	late	name

Use this code. **Write** the words.

a c d e f g k m n s t

1. _____

2. _____

3. _____

4. _____

5. _____

6. _____

7. _____

8. _____

9. _____

Write the missing letters. **Write** the word.

10. l__t _____

Home Activity Your child has been learning to spell words with long *a*. Ask your child to explain how all the list words are alike. (All have long *a*, and all end in *a*-consonant-*e*.)

Name _____

Words with Long *i*

Look at the word. **Say** it. **Listen** for the long *i* sound.

Write the word.	**Check** it.

1. like

2. ride

3. smile

4. time

5. white

6. bike

7. dime

8. hide

9. ice

10. kite

High-Frequency Words

11. who   12. work _____

Home Activity Your child is learning to spell words with the long *i* vowel sound. To practice at home, have your child write each word as you say it aloud.

© Pearson Education

Spelling Practice Book   **Unit 2 Week 3 Day 1** **33**

Name _____

Words with Long *i*

Spelling Words				
like	ride	smile	time	white
bike	dime	hide	ice	kite

Read the sentence. **Write** the words that rhyme.

They like the bike.

1. _____   2. _____

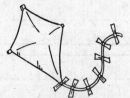

The kite is white.

3. _____   4. _____

Dad will use a dime this time.

5. _____   6. _____

Write the missing word.

7. The _____ makes me cold.

8. Did you walk or _____ ?

9. She has a big _____ on her face.

10. The cat likes to _____ from me.

ice
hide
ride
smile

School + Home   **Home Activity** Your child wrote words with the long *i* sound. Take turns with your child making up sentences containing the words. Spell the words aloud.

© Pearson Education

Words with Long *i*

Spelling Words				
like	ride	smile	time	white
bike	dime	hide	ice	kite

Choose a word to finish the sentence.
Fill in the circle. **Write** the word.

_____

1. The glass is full of ○ **ice**   ○ **bike**   ○ **dime**.   _____

2. Be there on   ○ **ride**   ○ **smile**   ○ **time**.   _____

3. Look at the   ○ **kite**   ○ **hide**   ○ **like**!   _____

4. It cost a   ○ **white**   ○ **dime**   ○ **ice**.   _____

5. Do you   ○ **time**   ○ **bike**   ○ **like** the color?   _____

6. You can ride my   ○ **bike**   ○ **ice**   ○ **time**.   _____

Read the word. **Write** the list word that means the opposite.

7. black _____   9. show _____

8. walk _____   10. frown _____

Home Activity Your child used spelling words to complete sentences. Have your child identify and write as many spelling words as possible to finish this sentence: *This is my_____.*

Name _____

Words with Long *i*

Write the list words in the puzzle.

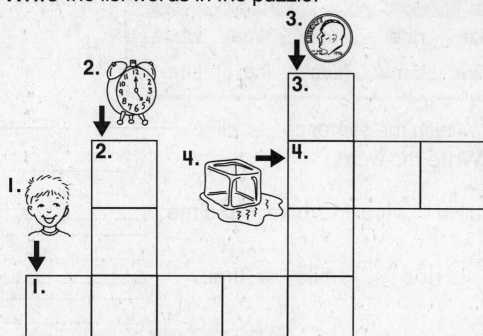

Spelling Words

like
ride
smile
time
white
bike
dime
hide
ice
kite

Draw lines to connect the words that rhyme. **Write** each word.

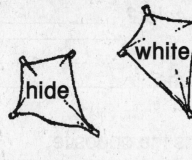

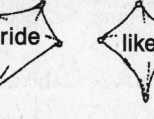

hide   white   kite   ride   like   bike

5. _____   6. _____   7. _____

8. _____   9. _____   10. _____

Home Activity Your child has been learning to spell words with long *i*. Draw large kite shapes. Have your child write long *i* words on them.

36 Unit 2 Week 3 **Day 4**   **Spelling Practice Book**

Name _____

Words with Long *o*

Look at the word. **Say** it. **Listen** for the long *o* sound.

Write the word.	**Check** it.

1. home

2. hope

3. rose

4. woke

5. those

6. bone

7. hose

8. joke

9. rode

10. stone

High-Frequency Words

11. there

12. together

Home Activity Your child is learning to spell words with the long o vowel sound. To practice at home, have your child spell each word out loud and then cover the word list and write each word. Then have your child check the word with the word list.

Name _____

Words with Long o

Spelling Words				
home	hope	rose	woke	those
bone	hose	joke	rode	stone

Write a list word for each clue.

_____

1. You use it to water the grass. _____

2. You live here. _____

3. It is a part of your body. _____

4. It makes you laugh. _____

5. It grows in a garden. _____

6. It hurts when it gets in your shoe. _____

Write the word that rhymes with each word.

7. smoke

_____

_____

8. rope

_____

_____

9. nose

_____

_____

10. code

_____

_____

those
woke
hope
rode

Home Activity Your child wrote words with long o. Work together to think of other long o words. Take turns making up clues for the new words and guessing them.

© Pearson Education

Name _____

Words with Long *o*

Spelling Words				
home	hope	rose	woke	those
bone	hose	joke	rode	stone

Read about Fluff and Puff. **Write** the missing list words.

Fluff and Puff live by a big **1.** _____ . One day Pup

dug for a **2.** _____ . Pup **3.** _____

Fluff and Puff. He entered their **4.** _____ . Now

5. _____ bunnies needed a new home. They had

little **6.** _____ . Puff **7.** _____ on

Fluff's back as they looked. Then Pup poked up over a

8. _____ bush. "I found a perfect home and that

is no **9.** _____ !" Pup had found a spot by the

garden **10.** _____ .

Home Activity Your child used spelling words in a story. Ask your child to write his or her own story, using some of the words.

Spelling Practice Book   **Unit 2 Week 4 Day 3** **39**

Words with Long *o*

Write the words.

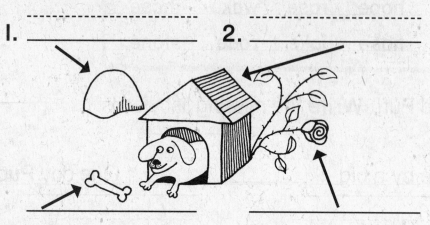

1. _____

2. _____

3. _____

4. _____

Write the missing letters. **Write** the list word.

5. **h** __ **p** __ _____

6. **th** __ _____

7. __ __ **d** __ _____

8. **j** __ __ __ _____

9. **h** __ **s** __ _____

10. **w** __ __ **k** __ _____

hope
woke
those
joke
rode
hose

Home Activity Your child has been learning to spell words with long *o*. Have your child think of and write words that rhyme with *nose* or *cone*.

40 Unit 2 Week 4 **Day 4**

Spelling Practice Book

Words with Long *u*

Look at the word. **Say** it. **Listen** for the long *u* sound.

Write the word.	**Check** it.

1. huge

2. June

3. rule

4. tube

5. use

6. cube

7. cute

8. flute

9. rude

10. mule

High-Frequency Words

11. water   12. under

Home Activity Your child is learning to spell words with the long *u* vowel sound. To practice at home, have your child write each word and then underline the long *u*. Then help him or her make up sentences with each word.

Words with Long *u*

Spelling Words				
huge	June	rule	tube	use
cube	cute	flute	rude	mule

Write the list word that names the picture.
Write a list word that rhymes.

1. _____   2. _____

3. _____   4. _____

5. _____   6. _____

Read the meaning. **Write** the list word.

June
use
rude
huge

7. very big   _____

8. not polite   _____

9. a month   _____

10. to work with something   _____

Home Activity Your child spelled words with the long *u* vowel sound. Ask your child to name the two letters that occur in every word. (*u* and *e*)

© Pearson Education

Words with Long *u*

Pick the word that finishes each sentence.
Write it on the line.

Spelling Words
huge
June
rule
tube
use
cube
cute
flute
rude
mule

_____

1. Put an ice _____ in the glass.

_____

2. I got to pet the _____ .

_____

3. You can _____ my pen.

_____

4. School is out in _____ .

_____

5. What a _____ kitten.

_____

6. Is there a _____ about that?

_____

7. This apple is _____ !

_____

8. Let's roll the ball down the _____ .

_____

9. I hear a _____ .

_____

10. Was she _____ to you?

School + Home **Home Activity** Your child completed sentences by spelling words with long *u*. Write "___u___e" and have your child fill in the blanks to spell a word.

© Pearson Education

Words with Long *u*

Spelling Words

huge	June	rule	tube	use
cube	cute	flute	rude	mule

Read the clue. **Write** the list word in the puzzle.

Across
3. after May
5. a pipe
6. animal

Down
1. a law
2. pretty
4. square box

Circle the word that is spelled correctly.

7. flute   flut   **8.** rude   rood

9. huje   huge   **10.** use   yuse

Home Activity Your child has been learning to spell words with long *u*. Take turns with your child naming and spelling the words.

© Pearson Education

Long e: *e, ee*

Look at the word. **Say** it. **Listen** for the long *e* sound.

Write the word.	**Check** it.
I. be	
2. feet	
3. he	
4. see	
5. we	
6. green	
7. me	
8. she	
9. tree	
10. week	

High-Frequency Words

II. some   12. family

School + Home

Home Activity Your child is learning to spell words with the long *e* vowel sound. To practice at home, have your child look at the word, say it, spell it, and then spell it with eyes closed.

Long e: e, ee

Spelling Words				
be	feet	he	see	we
green	me	she	tree	week

Write the list word that names the picture.

1. _____

2. _____

Write e or ee to finish the word. **Write** the word.

3. **sh**_____ _____

4. **h**_____ _____

5. **gr**_____**n** _____

6. **m**_____ _____

7. **s**_____ _____

8. **w**_____**k** _____

9. **w**_____ _____

10. **b**_____ _____

Home Activity Your child spelled words with the long e vowel sound. Ask your child to identify two different ways the sound is spelled in the list words. (e and ee)

© Pearson Education

Long e: e, ee

Spelling Words				
be	feet	he	see	we
green	me	she	tree	week

Read the story. **Write** the missing list words.

1. Dad helped _____ build a house for the birds.

2. A bird came the next _____ .

3. Soon _____ laid some eggs.

4. Dad held me up to _____ them.

5. There were three _____ eggs.

6. I asked if _____ could take one inside.

7. Dad said that would not _____ wise.

8. I knew _____ was right.

9. Dad put me back down on my _____ .

10. Now three little birds are in the _____ .

Home Activity Your child used spelling words to complete a story. Ask your child to use some of the list words in a story about an event in his or her life.

Long e: e, ee

Spelling Words				
be	feet	he	see	we
green	me	she	tree	week

Read the clue. **Write** the list word in the puzzle.

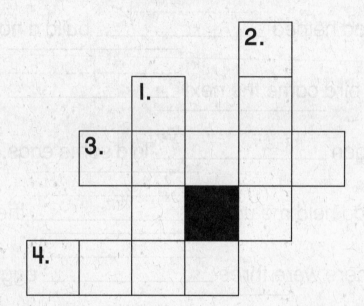

Down

1. large plant
2. seven days

Across

3. the color of grass
4. what you stand on

Circle the word that is spelled correctly. **Write** it.

5. b   be   _____

6. we   whe   _____

7. he   hee   _____

8. mee   me   _____

9. se   see   _____

10. she   shee   _____

Home Activity Your child has been learning to spell words with long e. Draw a tree and have your child write words with long e in the branches.

© Pearson Education

Long e and Long *i*: *y*

Look at the word. **Say** it. **Listen** for the long *e* or long *i* sound.

Write the word.	**Check** it.

1. my

2. by

3. try

4. any

5. body

6. fly

7. cry

8. lucky

9. silly

10. puppy

High-Frequency Words

11. things

12. always

© Pearson Education

School + Home

Home Activity Your child is learning to spell words in which the long *e* or long *i* sound is spelled *y*. To practice at home, have your child look at the word, say it, spell it, and then spell it with eyes closed.

Long e and Long i: y

Spelling Words				
my	by	try	any	body
fly	cry	lucky	silly	puppy

Write five list words that rhyme with **why**.

1. _cry_   2. _by_   3. _try_

4. _fly_   5. _cry_

Write the missing word.

any	silly	lucky	body	puppy

6. I have a _puppy_ named Spot.

7. He has a soft, furry _body_.

8. My pup acts _silly_.

9. Do you see _any_ dog toys?

10. I am _lucky_ to have a pup.

Home Activity Your child spelled words in which the long *e* or long *i* sound is spelled *y*. Ask your child to name the letter that is in every list word (*y*) and pronounce its sound (long *e* as in *puppy* or long *i* as in *fly*).

Spelling Practice Book

© Pearson Education

Long e and Long i: y

Spelling Words				
my	by	try	any	body
fly	cry	lucky	silly	puppy

Fill in the circle. **Write** the word.

1. Look at ○ fly ⊛ my ○ body bike.

my

2. I did not eat ⊛ any ○ try ○ by cake.

any

3. Did you ○ silly ○ puppy ⊛ cry?

cry

4. The song is ○ any ⊛ silly ○ my.

silly

5. She was ⊛ lucky ○ my ○ fly.

lucky

6. I ⊛ try ○ lucky ○ any very hard.

try

7. Bats can ○ silly ⊛ fly ○ my.

fly

8. Do you have a ⊛ puppy ○ cry ○ lucky?

puppy

9. His ○ any ○ by ⊛ body is strong.

body

10. Put it ○ my ○ fly ⊛ by the box.

by

Home Activity Your child wrote spelling words to complete sentences. Read a sentence from this page. Ask your child to spell the list word.

© Pearson Education

Long e and Long *i*: *y*

Write the letter **y**. Then write the word.

1. **fl**y _____ fly

2. **pupp**y _____ puppy

3. **cr**y _____ cry

4. **bod**y _____ body

5. **an**y _____ any

6. **sill**y _____ silly

7. **luck**y _____ lucky

Circle the words that rhyme with **fly**. **Write** the words.

any   try   body   silly   by my

8. _____ try   9. _____ by   10. _____ my

Home Activity Your child has been learning to spell words in which the long *e* or long *i* sound is spelled *y*. Have your child underline list words with a long *i* sound and circle list words with a long *e* sound.

52   Unit 3   Week 1   **Day 4**

Spelling Practice Book

Words with *ng* and *nk*

Look at the word. **Say** it. **Listen** for the *ng* or *nk* sound.

Write the word.   **Check** it.

1. bring

2. trunk

3. pink

4. bank

5. sang

6. wing

7. rink

8. blank

9. rang

10. sunk

High-Frequency Words

11. every   12. sure

© Pearson Education

School + Home

Home Activity Your child is learning to spell words with *ng* and *nk*. To practice at home, have your child spell each word. Then cover the word and ask your child to spell it again.

Words with *ng* and *nk*

Look at each picture.
Write two list words that rhyme.

Spelling Words
bring
trunk
pink
bank
sang
wing
rink
blank
rang
sunk

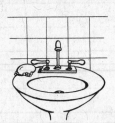

1. _rink_

2. _pink_

3. _bring_

4. _bwing_

5. _sunk_

6. _trunk_

Read the clue. **Write** the word.

7. You keep money in it.   7. _bank_

8. You did it to a bell.   8. _rang_

9. You did it to a song.   9. _sang_

10. You can write a word to fill it.   10. _blank_

Home Activity Your child spelled words ending in *ng* and *nk*. Have your child identify and spell each list word that ends with *nk*.

Words with *ng* and *nk*

Spelling Words				
bring	trunk	pink	bank	sang
wing	rink	blank	rang	sunk

Write the missing *ng* or *nk*. **Write** the word.

1. Did you skate at the **ri**___nk___ ? *pink*

2. Put the bag in the **tru**___nk___ . *trunk*

3. The bell **ra**___ng___ . *rang*

4. The boat has **su**___nk___ . *sunk*

5. We clapped as he **sa**___ng___ *sang*

6. I have a piggy **ba**___nk___ . *bank*

7. The bird hurt its **wi**___ng___ . *wing*

8. Did you paint it **pi**___nk___ ? *pink*

9. The page was **bla**___nk___ . *blank*

10. Do you know what to **bri**___ng___ ? *bring*

Home Activity Your child wrote spelling words to complete sentences. Have your child say and spell the list words with *ng*.

© Pearson Education

Words with *ng* and *nk*

Unscramble the letters to make a list word.
Write the word.

1. **k i n p**   1. _pink_

2. **r n g a**   2. _rang_

3. **g n i w**   3. _wing_

4. **n r i k**   4. _rink_

5. **r t n k u**   5. _trunk_

Write three list words that begin like 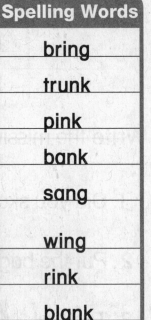 .

6. _bring_   7. _bank_   8. _blank_

Write two list words that begin like .

9. _sang_   10. _sunk_

Home Activity Your child has been learning to spell words with *ng* or *nk*. Have your child spell a list word and use it in a sentence.

© Pearson Education

Name _____

Adding -es

Look at the word. **Say** it. **Listen** for the ending.

Write the word.   **Check** it.

1. fix _____fix_____

2. fixes _____fixes_____

3. class _____class_____

4. classes _____classes_____

5. wish _____wish_____

6. wishes _____wishes_____

7. kiss _____kiss_____

8. kisses _____kisses_____

9. bus _____bus_____

10. buses _____Buses_____

High-Frequency Words

11. friends _____friends_____   12. very _____very_____

Home Activity Your child is learning to spell words that end with -es. To practice at home, have your child say each word. Help your child think of more words ending in -es.

Adding -es

Finish the list word. Then write the word that means more than one.

Spelling Words
fix
fixes
class
classes
wish
wishes
kiss
kisses
bus
buses

1. one **b** us

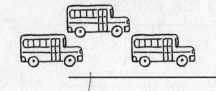

2. three buses

3. one **k** iss

4. three kisses

5. one **w** ish

6. three wishes

Write the missing word.

classes
fix
fixes
class

7. My class has ten boys.

8. Sam fixes clocks.

9. Do the music classes meet here?

10. Can you fix my bike?

Home Activity Your child spelled words that end with *-es*. Say a list word that does not end with *-es*. Ask your child to add *-es* and spell the new word.

© Pearson Education

Adding -es

Spelling Words				
fix	fixes	class	classes	wish
wishes	kiss	kisses	bus	buses

Read about a wish. **Write** the missing list words.

1. I _____*wish*_____ I could visit my aunt.

2. I would go by _____*buses*_____ .

3. I might need to ride on two or three _____*buses*_____ .

4. My aunt _____*fix*_____ hair in her shop.

5. She would _____*fix*_____ my hair.

6. She teaches art _____*classes*_____ , too.

7. I could go to a _____*class*_____ .

8. I would give my aunt a big _____*kiss*_____ .

9. She would give me lots of _____*kisses*_____

10. I hope my _____*wishes*_____ come true!

Home Activity Your child wrote spelling words to complete a story. Ask your child to write about a wish, using some of the list words.

Jan's New Home
REVIEW

Adding -es

Read the clues. **Write** the list words.

Spelling Words
fix
fixes
class
classes
wish
wishes
kiss
kisses
bus
buses

1. It rhymes with Gus.

_____
- - - - - - - - - - - -
_____

2. It rhymes with glass.

_____
- - - - - - - - - - - -
_____

3. It rhymes with fishes.

_____
- - - - - - - - - - - -
_____

4. It rhymes with dish.

_____
- - - - - - - - - - - -
_____

5. It rhymes with mix.

_____
- - - - - - - - - - - -
_____

6. It rhymes with miss.

_____
- - - - - - - - - - - -
_____

Add -es. **Write** the new word in the puzzle.

Down
7. bus
8. fix

Across
9. kiss
10. class

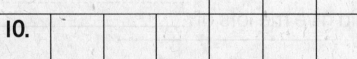

Home Activity Your child has been learning to add -es to words. Have your child write a list word that ends with -es. Then have your child cross out -es to make a different list word.

© Pearson Education

Adding -ed

Look at the word. **Say** it. **Listen** for the ending.

Write the word.	**Check** it.
1. ask	
2. asked	
3. plan	
4. planned	
5. help	
6. helped	
7. jog	
8. jogged	
9. call	
10. called	

High-Frequency Words

11. again _____ 12. soon _____

School + Home

Home Activity Your child is learning to spell words that end with *-ed*. To practice at home, have your child look at the word, say it, spell it, and then write the word. Help your child see how the word changes when adding *-ed*.

Name _____

Adding -ed

Write the list word to finish the chart.

Spelling Words

Base Word	-ed Word
1. _____	**asked**
2. **jog**	_____
3. _____	**helped**
4. **plan**	_____

Spelling Words:
ask
asked
plan
planned
help
helped
jog
jogged
call
called

Read the clues. Write the list word.

It rhymes with

It starts with **pl**.

5. _____

It rhymes with

It starts with **c**.

6. _____

It rhymes with

It starts with **j**.

7. _____

Write the list word that tells what happened in the past.

8. We can <u>ask</u> for paper. We _____ for paper.

9. I will <u>call</u> my friends. I _____ my friends.

10. He can <u>help</u>. He _____ .

School + Home

Home Activity Your child spelled words that do and do not end with *-ed*. Say a list word that does not end with *-ed*. Have your child say and spell the corresponding *-ed* word.

62 Unit 3 Week 4 **Day 2**

Spelling Practice Book

© Pearson Education

Adding -ed

Spelling Words				
ask	asked	plan	planned	help
helped	jog	jogged	call	called

Write the missing list words.

_____

1. He _____ if I could come.

_____

2. We have not _____ a trip.

_____

3. She _____ on the path.

_____

4. Has your mom _____ you back home?

_____

5. Jack _____ clean.

_____

6. Did you _____ your dog?

_____

7. I will _____ for more.

_____

8. Tom likes to _____ and run.

_____

9. Liz will help _____ .

_____

10. All can _____ us.

Home Activity Your child wrote words that end with -ed and their base words. Ask your child to find two words in which the final consonant was doubled before adding -ed (plan/planned, jog/jogged).

Adding -ed

Read the base word. **Write** the *-ed* word in the puzzle.

Spelling Words

ask
asked
plan
planned
help
helped
jog
jogged
call
called

Across

2. help   4. call
5. jog

Down

1. ask
3. plan

Circle the word that is spelled correctly.

6. plan   plann   7. asc   ask

8. cal   call   9. help   halp

10. jog   joj

Home Activity Your child has been learning to add *-ed* to base words. Have your child write a list word that ends with *-ed*. Then have your child cross out the ending (*-ed* or *consonant* + *-ed*) to find the base word.

Name _____

Words with *er*, *ir*, *ur*

Look at the word. **Say** it. **Look** for the vowel spelling.

Write the word.	**Check** it.

1. her

2. first

3. bird

4. girl

5. burn

6. were

7. shirt

8. fur

9. hurt

10. sir

High-Frequency Words

11. visit

12. done

Home Activity Your child is learning to spell words with *er*, *ir*, and *ur*. To practice at home, have your child say each word and point to the vowel spelling.

Words with *er*, *ir*, *ur*

Spelling Words				
her	first	bird	girl	burn
were	shirt	fur	hurt	sir

Read the clues. **Write** the list word.

It starts like

It rhymes with **bur**.
_____

1. _____

It starts like

It rhymes with **dirt**.
_____

2. _____

It starts like

It rhymes with **turn**.
_____

3. _____

Write the list word that means the opposite.

4. last _____

5. boy _____

6. heal _____

7. him _____

Write the missing list word.

sir	were	bird

8. We saw a _____ .

9. May I help you, _____ ?

10. We _____ at a pond.

Home Activity Your child spelled words with *er*, *ir*, and *ur*. Have your child circle these letter combinations in the list words.

I'm a Caterpillar
CONNECT TO WRITING

Words with *er, ir, ur*

Circle the word that is spelled correctly. **Write** it.

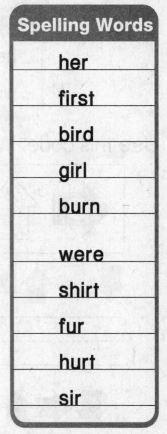

Spelling Words

her

first

bird

girl

burn

were

shirt

fur

hurt

sir

1. I like your ____.

   shert   shirt   shurt   _____

2. I knew where you ____.

   were   wir   wure   _____

3. Meet the new ____.

   gerl   girl   gurl   _____

4. Let the candle ____.

   bern   birn   burn   _____

5. Judy said, "Yes, ____."

   ser   sir   sur   _____

6. Look at the ____.

   berd   bird   burd   _____

7. Can I be ____?

   ferst   first   furst   _____

8. His dog has black ____.

   fer   fure   fur   _____

9. Did you get ____?

   hert   hirt   hurt   _____

10. I played a game with ____.

    her   hir   hur   _____

Home Activity Your child used spelling words in sentences. Help your child make up a new sentence for each spelling word.

© Pearson Education

Name _____

Words with *er, ir, ur*

Spelling Words				
her	first	bird	girl	burn
were	shirt	fur	hurt	sir

Use this code. **Write** the words.

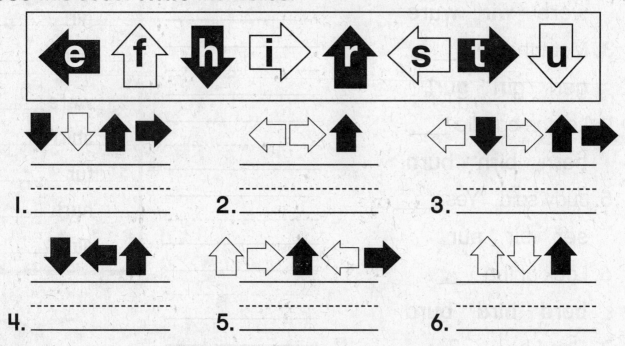

1. _____

2. _____

3. _____

4. _____

5. _____

6. _____

Draw a line through the word that does not match.
Then **write** the word that matches.

_____

7. were   where   were   _____

8. bird   bird   bid   _____

9. grill   girl   girl   _____

10. burn   turn   burn   _____

Home Activity Your child has been learning to spell words with *er, ir,* and *ur*. Write a list word, but replace the letter before *r* with a blank (b__rd). Ask your child to correctly fill in the blank.

© Pearson Education

Name _____

Adding -er and -est

Look at the word. **Say** it. **Listen** for the word ending.

Write the word.   **Check** it.

1. bigger

2. biggest

3. faster

4. fastest

5. slower

6. slowest

7. shorter

8. shortest

9. sadder

10. saddest

High-Frequency Words

11. good-bye   12. before

School + Home

Home Activity Your child is learning to spell words that end with -er and -est. To practice at home, have your child look at the word, say it, spell it, and then spell it with eyes closed.

Adding -er and -est

Spelling Words				
bigger	biggest	faster	fastest	slower
slowest	shorter	shortest	sadder	saddest

Look at the pictures. **Write** list words that end with *-er* and *-est*.

short

1. _____ 2. _____

fast

3. _____ 4. _____

big

5. _____ 6. _____

Write a list word that rhymes with the underlined word.

7. The <u>mower</u> runs _____ uphill.

8. The <u>lowest</u> branches move _____ in the wind.

9. His face grew _____ as he put away the <u>ladder</u>.

10. This is the _____ and the <u>maddest</u> he's ever been.

Home Activity Your child spelled words that end with *-er* and *-est*. Say a base word, such as *big*. Ask your child to say and spell the *-er* and *-est* words (*bigger*, *biggest*).

Adding -er and -est

Spelling Words				
bigger	biggest	faster	fastest	slower
slowest	shorter	shortest	sadder	saddest

Add -er or -est. **Write** the list word.

1. The biggest dog was the slow___.

_____

2. The fast___ runner will win the race.

_____

3. My bat is short___ than yours.

_____

4. I need some bigg___ shoes.

_____

5. That is the sadd___ clown I've ever seen.

_____

6. You walk fast___ than I do.

_____

7. The story made her feel even sadd___.

_____

8. This is the world's bigg___ pizza.

_____

9. Our team was slow___ than yours.

_____

10. Did you find the very short___ path?

_____

Home Activity Your child wrote spelling words to complete sentences. Have your child circle the base word in each spelling word.

Adding **-er** and **-est**

Spelling Words				
bigger	biggest	faster	fastest	slower
slowest	shorter	shortest	sadder	saddest

Finish the list words.

1. **sl** _ _ _ **r**

2. **sh** _ _ _ **r**

3. **sl** _ _ _ **s** _

4. **sh** _ _ _ **s** _

5. **s** _ _ **d** _ _ _

6. **b** _ _ _ _ _ **t**

7. **b** _ _ _ **e** _

8. **s** _ _ _ _ _ **s** _

Write the missing words.

Froggy   Hopper

9. Hopper is _____ than Froggy.

10. Hopper is _____ .

| fastest |
| faster |

Home Activity Your child has been learning to spell words ending in -er and -est. Play a game with your child by tossing a coin onto this page. Read the list word that is closest to where the coin lands and have your child spell it. Take turns.

72 Unit 3 Week 6 **Day 4**   **Spelling Practice Book**

Name _____

Long *a*: *ai*, *ay*

Look at the word. **Say** it. **Listen** for the long *a* sound.

Write the word.	**Check** it.

1. train

2. way

3. tail

4. play

5. day

6. may

7. rain

8. gray

9. mail

10. afraid

High-Frequency Words

11. about

12. would

School + Home

Home Activity Your child is learning to spell words with the long *a* sound spelled *ai* and *ay*. To practice at home, have your child look at the word, say it, and write the words spelled with *ai* in one column and *ay* in another column.

Long *a*: *ai*, *ay*

Spelling Words				
train	way	tail	play	day
may	rain	gray	mail	afraid

Write the words in ABC order.

tail	afraid	way	may	gray	day

1. _____

2. _____

3. _____

4. _____

5. _____

6. _____

Draw a line from the word to its picture. **Write** the word.

mail

rain

train

play

7. _____

8. _____

9. _____

10. _____

Home Activity Your child spelled words with the long *a* sound spelled *ai* and *ay*. Have your child circle *ai* and *ay* in the spelling words.

© Pearson Education

Long *a*: *ai*, *ay*

Spelling Words				
train	way	tail	play	day
may	rain	gray	mail	afraid

Read about a dog. **Write** the missing list words.

1. I have a _____ dog.

2. He is _____ of storms.

3. He hides when it starts to _____ .

4. He barks when he hears a _____ .

5. Could he learn a _____ to play catch?

6. Could he fetch the _____ ?

7. I think he _____ learn.

8. Look at him wag his _____ .

9. He wants to _____ .

10. I will train him some other _____ .

Home Activity Your child wrote spelling words to complete a story about a dog. Have your child make up a story, using some of the list words.

Name _____

Long *a*: *ai*, *ay*

Spelling Words				
train	way	tail	play	day
may	rain	gray	mail	afraid

Underline the words that rhyme. **Write** the words.

Whose tail is on the mail?

1. _____

2. _____

Is there a train in the rain?

3. _____

4. _____

When may we play?

5. _____

6. _____

Circle the word that is spelled correctly.

7. gray   gra   8. day   dai

9. afrayd   afraid   10. waye   way

Home Activity Your child has been learning to spell words with the long *a* sound spelled *ai* and *ay*. Help your child think of and spell words that rhyme with some of the list words.

© Pearson Education

Name _____

Long e: *ea*

Look at the word. **Say** it. **Listen** for the long *e* sound.

Write the word.   **Check** it.

1. eat

2. sea

3. each

4. team

5. please

6. dream

7. treat

8. beach

9. clean

10. lean

High-Frequency Words

11. colors   12. sign

School + Home

Home Activity Your child is learning to spell words with the long *e* sound spelled *ea*. To practice at home, have your child say the word, find the letters *ea*, and then write the word.

© Pearson Education

Long e: ea

Spelling Words				
eat	sea	each	team	please
dream	treat	beach	clean	lean

Write two list words that rhyme with the picture.

1. _____

2. _____

3. _____

4. _____

5. _____

6. _____

Write the missing words.

Spelling Words	
sea	please
team	dream

7. My _____ won!

8. I _____ about trips.

9. I love the _____ .

10. Can we _____ go there?

Home Activity Your child spelled words with the long e sound spelled ea. Ask your child to name the two letters that appear in every spelling word (ea).

78 Unit 4 Week 2 **Day 2**

Spelling Practice Book

© Pearson Education

Name _____

Long e: *ea*

Spelling Words				
eat	sea	each	team	please
dream	treat	beach	clean	lean

Write the missing letters. **Write** the word.

1. Is it time to **ea**___ ? _____

2. Let's go to the ___**ea**___ ___ . _____

3. I can ___ ___**ea**___ the porch. _____

4. Don't ___**ea**___ over too far. _____

5. I had a ___**ea**___ last night. _____

6. Will you ___ ___**ea**___ sit? _____

7. Fish live in the ___**ea** . _____

8. My ___**ea**___ lost! _____

9. I read **ea**___ ___ story. _____

10. Give the pup a ___ ___**ea**___ . _____

Home Activity Your child wrote spelling words to complete sentences. Read a sentence on this page and have your child spell the list word.

© Pearson Education

Long *e*: *ea*

Write list words in the puzzle.

Across
2. chew food
4. not dirty

Down
1. sandy shore
3. ocean
5. thin

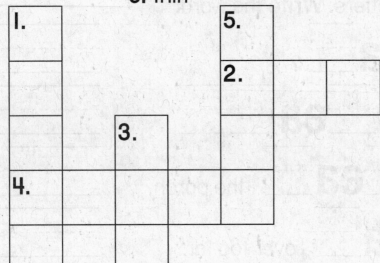

Spelling Words
eat
sea
each
team
please
dream
treat
beach
clean
lean

Draw lines through all the **i**'s and **k**'s. **Write** the word that is left.

6. **t i e k a k m i** _____

7. **p l i e a k k s i e** _____

8. **k t i r e k a k i t** _____

9. **e i a k c i k h** _____

10. **d i r k i e a m** _____

School + Home

Home Activity Your child has been learning to spell words with the long *e* sound spelled *ea*. Have your child identify and spell the three words he or she found most difficult.

© Pearson Education

Mister Bones
WRITE AND CHECK

Long o: oa, ow

Look at the word. **Say** it. **Listen** for the long *o* sound.

Write the word.	**Check** it.
1. boat	
2. road	
3. snow	
4. row	
5. yellow	
6. loaf	
7. coat	
8. soap	
9. blow	
10. pillow	

High-Frequency Words

11. once _____ 12. wild _____

Home Activity Your child is learning to spell words with the long *o* vowel sound spelled *oa* and *ow*. To practice at home, have your child pronounce each word, note the spelling of the long *o* sound, and then spell the word with eyes closed.

© Pearson Education

Name _____

Long o: *oa, ow*

Read the clues. **Write** the word.

Spelling Words
boat
road
snow
row
yellow
loaf
coat
soap
blow
pillow

It rhymes with **willow**.
You sleep on it.

_____

1. _____

It rhymes with **goat**.
It goes in water.

_____

2. _____

It rhymes with **mow**.
It's cold and white.

_____

3. _____

It rhymes with **fellow**.
It's a color.

_____

4. _____

It rhymes with **load**.
Cars go on it.

_____

5. _____

It rhymes with **goat**.
You wear it.

_____

6. _____

Write the missing word.

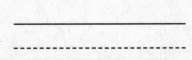

7. I like to ____ bubbles.

8. Did you ____ the boat?

9. I got ____ in my eyes.

10. The ____ of bread is warm.

School + Home

Home Activity Your child spelled words with the long *o* vowel sound spelled *oa* and *ow*. Have your child underline *oa* and *ow* in the spelling words.

© Pearson Education

Long o: oa, ow

Spelling Words				
boat	road	snow	row	yellow
loaf	coat	soap	blow	pillow

Write the missing list word.

1. Lemons are _____ .

2. Wash with _____ .

3. Would you like to ride in our _____ ?

4. I sleep on a soft _____ .

5. Wear your _____ .

6. He will _____ the boat.

7. Please buy a _____ of bread.

8. Is it cold enough to _____ ?

9. This _____ has a lot of stop signs.

10. Can you _____ up this balloon?

Home Activity Your child wrote spelling words to complete sentences. Ask your child to create a sentence using one or two of the spelling words.

Long *o*: *oa*, *ow*

Spelling Words				
boat	road	snow	row	yellow
loaf	coat	soap	blow	pillow

Write the list word that belongs in the group.

blanket sheet

1. _____

blue red

3. _____

jacket sweater

5. _____

rain sleet

2. _____

street highway

4. _____

ship ocean liner

6. _____

Circle the word that matches. **Write** it.

_____

7. **row**   bow   row

_____

8. **loaf**   load   loaf

_____

9. **blow**   blow   flow

_____

10. **soap**   soak   soap

_____

Home Activity Your child has been learning words with the long *o* vowel sound spelled *oa* and *ow*. Give clues about a word. Can your child guess and spell the word?

Spelling Practice Book

Long *i*: *ie*, *igh*

Look at the word. **Say** it. **Listen** for the long *i* sound.

	Write the word.	**Check** it.
I. lie		
2. tie		
3. high		
4. might		
5. right		
6. night		
7. bright		
8. light		
9. pie		
10. tight		

High-Frequency Words

II. above _____ 12. laugh _____

School + Home **Home Activity** Your child is learning to spell words with the long *i* sound spelled *ie* and *igh*. To practice at home, have your child say the word, tell how the long *i* sound is spelled, and then spell the word with eyes closed.

© Pearson Education

Long *i*: *ie*, *igh*

Spelling Words				
lie	tie	high	might	right
night	bright	light	pie	tight

Write the list word that names the picture.

1. _____   2. _____   3. _____

Write the list word that means the same as the underlined word.

4. These gloves are too <u>snug</u>.

4. _____

5. What is the <u>correct</u> answer?

5. _____

6. The wall is <u>tall</u>.

6. _____

7. We pulled with all our <u>strength</u>.

7. _____

8. Let's wait until <u>evening</u>.

8. _____

9. She is very <u>smart</u>.

9. _____

10. I would not tell a <u>fib</u>.

10. _____

School + Home

Home Activity Your child spelled words with the long *i* sound spelled *ie* and *igh*. Have your child circle *ie* and *igh* in the spelling words.

© Pearson Education

Long *i*: *ie*, *igh*

Spelling Words				
lie	tie	high	might	right
night	bright	light	pie	tight

Write a list word to finish the sentence.

1. You are r____.

2. Turn on the l____.

3. I love to eat p____!

4. Will you wear a t____?

5. The roof is h____.

6. It's a cold n____.

7. The stars are b____.

8. My belt is too t____.

9. Do not tell a l____.

10. Pam m____ come over.

1. _____

2. _____

3. _____

4. _____

5. _____

6. _____

7. _____

8. _____

9. _____

10. _____

© Pearson Education

Home Activity Your child wrote spelling words to complete sentences. Help your child use the list words in new sentences.

Name _____

Long *i*: *ie*, *igh*

Draw a line through three rhyming list words in a row. **Write** the words.

might	read	lie
row	tie	tight
pie	loaf	road

pie	right	coat
sled	tight	low
blue	might	high

1. _____
2. _____
3. _____
4. _____
5. _____
6. _____

Spelling Words

lie
tie
high
might
right
night
bright
light
pie
tight

Write the missing words.

7. It is up _____ .

8. It looks _____ .

9. You see it at _____ .

10. It looks like a _____ .

night	bright
light	high

Home Activity Your child has been learning to spell words with the long *i* sound spelled *ie* and *igh*. Say a list word. Ask your child how the long *i* sound is spelled (*ie* or *igh*).

© Pearson Education

Name _____

Compound Words

Look at the word. **Say** it. **Listen** for two short words.

	Write the word.	**Check** it.
1. backpack		
2. outside		
3. baseball		
4. herself		
5. flashlight		
6. bluebird		
7. lunchbox		
8. suitcase		
9. inside		
10. brainstorm		

High-Frequency Words

11. picture _____ 12. remember _____

Home Activity Your child is learning to spell compound words. To practice at home, have your child look at the word, write it on a piece of paper, and draw a line between the two words that make up the compound word.

© Pearson Education

Compound Words

Name _____

Write the list word that names the picture.

1. _____   2. _____

3. _____   4. _____

5. _____   6. _____

Write the last part of the compound word.
Write the compound word.

7. in _____   _____

8. her _____   _____

9. brain _____   _____

10. out _____   _____

Home Activity Your child spelled compound words. Have your child name the two words in each compound word.

© Pearson Education

Compound Words

Spelling Words				
backpack	outside	baseball	herself	flashlight
bluebird	lunchbox	suitcase	inside	brainstorm

Read about some good friends. **Write** the missing list words.

1. Ellie and I went **o**_____ .

2. Ellie had a **f**_____ .

3. We saw **b**_____ feathers.

4. We looked **i**_____ a hollow tree.

5. Next, we played **b**_____ .

6. Then we got a snack out of my **l**_____ .

7. We got juice out of Ellie's **b**_____ .

8. Ellie drank three boxes of juice by **h**_____ .

9. She could drink a **s**_____ full of juice!

10. We will **b**_____ something else to do.

School + Home

Home Activity Your child used spelling words to complete a story about friends. Ask your child to tell about a friend, using some of the list words.

© Pearson Education

Name _____

Compound Words

Connect two parts to make a list word.
Write the compound word.

1. in   storm   1. _____

2. her   side   2. _____

3. brain   light   3. _____

4. flash   self   4. _____

5. suit   bird   5. _____

6. blue   case   6. _____

Circle the word that is spelled correctly.

7. lunchbox   lonchbox   8. owtside   outside

9. backpack   back pack   10. basball   baseball

Home Activity Your child has been learning to spell compound words. Help your child brainstorm other compound words.

92 Unit 4 Week 5 **Day 4**

Spelling Practice Book

© Pearson Education

Suffixes: -ly, -ful

Look at the word. **Say** it. **Listen** for two short sounds.

Write the word.	**Check** it.

1. slowly

2. careful

3. quickly

4. useful

5. painful

6. playful

7. sadly

8. gladly

9. nicely

10. wonderful

High-Frequency Words

11. because

12. across

School + Home

Home Activity Your child is learning to spell words with the suffixes -ly and -ful. To practice at home, have your child look at the word, say the base word and the suffix, and then spell the word.

Suffixes: *-ly, -ful*

Spelling Words				
slowly	careful	quickly	useful	painful
playful	sadly	gladly	nicely	wonderful

Write the list word that means the same as the underlined words.

1. She said good-bye <u>in a sad way</u>.

1. _____

2. We had a <u>very good</u> time.

2. _____

3. Be <u>alert</u> when playing ball.

3. _____

4. The twins play <u>in a nice way</u>.

4. _____

5. Her foot was <u>full of pain</u>.

5. _____

6. I will <u>be happy to</u> help.

6. _____

7. The hamsters are <u>full of play</u>.

7. _____

8. Drive <u>in a slow way</u>.

8. _____

9. My pen is still <u>full of use</u>.

9. _____

10. He finished his work <u>in a fast way</u>.

10. _____

Home Activity Your child spelled words with the suffixes *-ly* and *-ful*. Ask your child to explain what each suffix means (suffix *-ly* means in a ___ way; suffix *-ful* means full of ___).

© Pearson Education

Suffixes: *-ly, -ful*

Spelling Words				
slowly	careful	quickly	useful	painful
playful	sadly	gladly	nicely	wonderful

Write the suffix **-ly** or **-ful**. **Write** the word.

_____

1. I went glad_____ .

_____

2. The swimmers were care_____ .

_____

3. It is a wonder_____ party.

_____

4. A cell phone is very use_____ .

_____

5. Mia plays nice_____ .

_____

6. We quick_____ shut the door.

_____

7. That's a play_____ kitten.

_____

8. Cook the stew slow_____ .

_____

9. A bee sting can be pain_____ .

_____

10. He left sad_____ .

Home Activity Your child used spelling words to complete sentences. Read a sentence and have your child spell the list word.

© Pearson Education

Suffixes: *-ly, -ful*

Spelling Words				
slowly	careful	quickly	useful	painful
playful	sadly	gladly	nicely	wonderful

Circle the word that is spelled correctly.

1. sadly   sady   2. galadly   gladly

3. quickly   quikly   4. wondrful   wonderful

Write the list words in the puzzle.

Across
7. in a nice way
9. in a slow way
10. full of use

Down
5. full of pain
6. full of play
8. not careless

Home Activity Your child has been learning to spell words with the suffixes *-ly* and *-ful*. Say a base word. Ask your child to add *-ly* or *-ful* and say and spell the new word.

© Pearson Education

Vowel Sound in *how*

Look at the word. **Say** it. **Listen** for the vowel sound.

Write the word.	**Check** it.

1. how

2. town

3. down

4. now

5. brown

6. cow

7. clown

8. frown

9. crowd

10. growl

High-Frequency Words

11. eyes   12. never

Home Activity Your child is learning to spell words with the vowel sound in *how*. To practice at home, have your child say the word, write the word, and circle *ow* in each word.

© Pearson Education

Spelling Practice Book   Unit 5 Week 1 **Day 1** **97**

Name _____

Vowel Sound in *how*

Spelling Words				
how	town	down	now	brown
cow	clown	frown	crowd	growl

Name the picture. **Write** a list word.

1. _____   2. _____   3. _____

Circle the correct word in the phrase. **Write** the word.

4. up and   **down**   **cow**   4. _____

5. a brown   **cow**   **now**   5. _____

6. **town**   **how**   about that   6. _____

7. lost in the   **crowd**   **down**   7. _____

8. the   **brown**   **growl**   of the lion   8. _____

9. **clown**   **now**   and then   9. _____

10. wipe off that   **frown**   **down**   10. _____

Home Activity Your child spelled words with the vowel sound in *how*. Ask your child to name two letters common to all the spelling words. (*ow*)

© Pearson Education

Vowel Sound in *how*

Spelling Words				
how	town	down	now	brown
cow	clown	frown	crowd	growl

Write the missing list word.

_____

1. We saw him milk a _____ .

2. Don't get lost in the _____ .

3. Her hair is _____ .

4. Do you know _____ to skate?

5. I heard the dog _____ .

6. We have a park in our _____ .

7. Let's go _____ the slide.

8. The best time is _____ .

9. The _____ was funny.

10. He had a _____ on his face.

Home Activity Your child wrote spelling words to complete sentences. Have your child spell a list word and use it in a sentence.

© Pearson Education

Vowel Sound in *how*

Spelling Words				
how	town	down	now	brown
cow	clown	frown	crowd	growl

Unscramble the letters. **Write** the list word.

1. l o c n w   1. _____

2. w o h   2. _____

3. b n r o w   3. _____

4. w l g r o   4. _____

5. o w c   5. _____

6. n t w o   6. _____

7. o n w   7. _____

Write the missing words.

8. The _____ had to wait in a long line.

9. There was no place to sit _____ .

10. Everyone began to _____ .

Home Activity Your child has been learning to spell words with the vowel sound in *how*. Give clues about a word. Ask your child to guess and spell the word.

© Pearson Education

Name _____

Vowel Sound in *out*

Look at the word. **Say** it. **Listen** for the vowel sound.

Write the word.   **Check** it.

1. mouth _____   _____

2. house _____   _____

3. found _____   _____

4. our _____   _____

5. out _____   _____

6. cloud _____   _____

7. ouch _____   _____

8. shout _____   _____

9. round _____   _____

10. count _____   _____

High-Frequency Words

11. should _____   12. loved _____

School + Home   **Home Activity** Your child is learning to spell words with the vowel sound in *out*. To practice at home, have your child pronounce each word, study the spelling of the word, and then write the word.

Vowel Sound in *out*

Read the clue. **Write** the list word.

It starts with **h**, and it rhymes with **mouse**.

1. _____

It starts with **cl**, and it rhymes with **loud**.

2. _____

It starts with **sh**, and it rhymes with **pout**.

3. _____

It starts with **o**, and it rhymes with **couch**.

4. _____

Write the missing list word.

5. Look at _____ pups.

6. We _____ them last week.

7. Can you _____ them?

8. One pup wants to get _____ .

9. He put an ice cube in his _____ .

10. The dime is _____ .

School + Home

Home Activity Your child spelled words with the vowel sound in *out*. Ask your child to name two letters common to all the spelling words. (*ou*)

© Pearson Education

Vowel Sound in *out*

Spelling Words				
mouth	house	found	our	out
cloud	ouch	shout	round	count

Read about finding bugs. **Write** the missing list words.

1. We _____ some bugs.

2. They are _____ .

3. Let's _____ them.

4. One got in my _____ .

5. Did you _____ ?

6. I said _____ .

7. I spit it _____ .

8. Look at that _____ !

9. Will _____ bugs get wet?

10. Let's take them in the _____ .

Home Activity Your child used spelling words to complete sentences. Read a sentence on this page. Have your child spell the list word.

Vowel Sound in *out*

Spelling Words
mouth   house   found   our   out
cloud   ouch   shout   round   count

Write the words in the puzzle.

1. | | O | U | | |

2. | | O | U | | |

3. | | O | U | | |

4. | | | O | U | |

cloud
ouch
out
mouth

Connect the matching list words.

5. found

6. round

7. our

9. shout

found

8. house

house

10. count

count

shout

round

our

Home Activity Your child has been learning to spell words with the vowel sound in *out*. Draw a big butterfly. Have your child write the list words on the wings.

Spelling Practice Book

Vowel Sounds in *book* and *moon*

Look at the word. **Say** it. **Listen** for the vowel sound.

	Write the word.	**Check** it.
1. book		
2. moon		
3. took		
4. food		
5. look		
6. pool		
7. zoo		
8. noon		
9. good		
10. foot		

High-Frequency Words

11. instead	12. another

Home Activity Your child is learning to spell words with the vowel sounds in *book* and *moon*. To practice at home, have your child look at the word and spell it out loud. Then cover the word and have your child write the word.

Vowel Sounds in *book* and *moon*

Circle the words in the box that rhyme. **Write** them.

foot	took
look	pool

1. _____
2. _____

foot	moon
book	noon

3. _____
4. _____

Spelling Words

book

moon

took

food

look

pool

zoo

noon

good

foot

Write a word that often goes with the list word.

5. bad   5. _____

6. hand   6. _____

7. drink   7. _____

Write the missing list word.

8. Greg wants to read a _____ .

9. Ann wants to swim at the _____ .

10. Joe wants to feed deer at the _____ .

Home Activity Your child spelled words with the vowel sound in *book* and *moon*. Ask your child to pronounce each list word and identify the vowel sound.

© Pearson Education

Dot & Jabber
CONNECT TO WRITING

Vowel Sounds in *book* and *moon*

Spelling Words				
book	moon	took	food	look
pool	zoo	noon	good	foot

Choose a word to finish the sentence.
Fill in the circle. **Write** the word.

1. I ◯ took ◯ look ◯ foot   a sack lunch.

2. Read the ◯ took ◯ zoo ◯ book.

3. My ◯ foot ◯ noon ◯ took   got wet.

4. We need more ◯ noon ◯ food ◯ look.

5. Bears are at the ◯ zoo ◯ moon ◯ foot.

6. That is ◯ look ◯ good ◯ took   news.

7. We swim in the ◯ noon ◯ foot ◯ pool.

8. The ◯ look ◯ took ◯ moon   is bright.

9. Did you ◯ pool ◯ look ◯ zoo   at it?

10. I must leave at ◯ noon ◯ took ◯ moon.

Home Activity Your child wrote spelling words to complete sentences. Have your child create a sentence using three or more list words.

© Pearson Education

Vowel Sounds in *book* and *moon*

Write the missing letters.

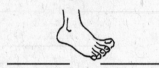

1. ___ **oo** ___

2. ___ **oo** ___

3. ___ **oo** ___

4. ___ **oo** ___

Write the list word in the puzzle.

Across

6. 12:00

8. you eat this

9. see

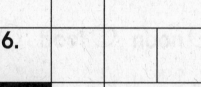

Down

5. not bad

7. opposite of *gave*

10. animals live there

School + Home

Home Activity Your child has been learning to spell words with the vowel sounds in *book* and *moon*. Write *oo* and pronounce a list word. Have your child add letters to spell the word. Continue with other list words.

© Pearson Education

Vowel Sound in *boy*

Look at the word. **Say** it. **Listen** for the vowel sound.

Write the word.   **Check** it.

1. oil

2. soil

3. voice

4. point

5. boy

6. boil

7. coin

8. oink

9. toy

10. join

High-Frequency Words

11. against _____   12. heavy _____

School + Home **Home Activity** Your child is learning to spell words with the vowel sound in *boy* spelled *oi* and *oy*. To practice at home, have your child look at the word, say it, and write it on a piece of paper. Then have your child spell the word.

Spelling Practice Book   **Unit 5 Week 4 Day 1** **109**

Vowel Sound in *boy*

Spelling Words				
oil	soil	voice	point	boy
boil	coin	oink	toy	join

Circle the rhyming words in each row. **Write** them.

toy   oil   boil   1. _____   2. _____

coin   join   boil   3. _____   4. _____

toy   soil   boy   5. _____   6. _____

Read the sentence. **Write** a list word that means the same as the underlined word.

7. Do you hear the big pig <u>squeal</u>?   7. _____

8. The farmer's <u>sound</u> is loud.   8. _____

9. The post has a sharp <u>end</u>.   9. _____

10. The <u>ground</u> is very muddy.   10. _____

School + Home

Home Activity Your child spelled words with the vowel sound in *book* and *moon*. Ask your child to pronounce each list word and identify the vowel sound.

Spelling Practice Book

Name _____

Vowel Sound in *boy*

Spelling Words

oil	soil	voice	point	boy
boil	coin	oink	toy	join

Circle a word to finish the sentence. **Write** the word.

1. Cover the seeds with   **soil**   **toy**.

2. He put a   **voice**   **coin**   in his bank.

3. I will   **boil**   **point**   to the answer.

4. Is this wagon your   **soil**   **toy**?

5. The pigs began to   **oink**   **coin**.

6. Did you   **voice**   **join**   the club?

7. I saw a   **boy**   **oil**   in the hall.

8. She spoke in a soft   **coin**   **voice**.

9. Did the water   **boil**   **zoo**?

10. Dad put   **join**   **oil**   in the car.

© Pearson Education

Home Activity Your child wrote spelling words to complete sentences. Have your child identify and spell the five list words that are most difficult for him or her.

Vowel Sound in *boy*

Spelling Words				
oil	soil	voice	point	boy
boil	coin	oink	toy	join

Write these words in ABC order.

| soil |
| voice |
| point |
| toy |

1. _____   2. _____

3. _____   4. _____

Use this code. **Write** the words.

5. _____   6. _____   7. _____

8. _____   9. _____   10. _____

Home Activity Your child has been learning to spell words with the vowel sound in *boy* spelled *oi* and *oy*. Help your child brainstorm other words with *oi* and *oy*.

© Pearson Education

112 Unit 5 Week 4 **Day 4**

Spelling Practice Book

Vowel Sound in *saw*

Look at the word. **Say** it. **Listen** for the vowel sound.

Write the word.	**Check** it.

1. saw
2. draw
3. crawl
4. straw
5. law
6. jaw
7. paw
8. lawn
9. yawn
10. hawk

High-Frequency Words

11. through _____   12. science _____

School + Home

Home Activity Your child is learning to spell words with the vowel sound in *saw*. To practice at home, have your child say the word, write it, and then check the spelling.

Vowel Sound in *saw*

Write a list word that belongs in the group.

Spelling Words
saw
draw
crawl
straw
law
jaw
paw
lawn
yawn
hawk

1. jay, eagle, _____

2. hammer, sandpaper, _____

3. skull, ribs, _____

4. skip, walk, _____

5. paint, sketch, _____

6. rule, order, _____

Write the missing words.

7. I sat on the _____ .

8. My dog sat on some _____ .

9. He put his _____ on my leg.

10. We both began to _____ .

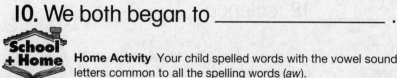

School + Home **Home Activity** Your child spelled words with the vowel sound in *saw*. Have your child name the two letters common to all the spelling words (*aw*).

114 Unit 5 Week 5 **Day 2**

Spelling Practice Book

© Pearson Education

Vowel Sound in *saw*

Spelling Words				
saw	draw	crawl	straw	law
jaw	paw	lawn	yawn	hawk

Write the missing list word.

1. The _____ says to wear seatbelts.

2. The baby is learning to _____.

3. Did you mow the _____?

4. Look at that _____ fly.

5. My _____ is sore.

6. Let's _____ a picture.

7. We _____ a snake.

8. My cat has one white _____.

9. She drank through a _____.

10. I tried not to _____.

Home Activity Your child wrote spelling words to complete sentences. Help your child make silly sentences by substituting other list words in the sentences. For example: The **hawk** says to wear seatbelts.

Spelling Practice Book

Unit 5 Week 5 **Day 3** **115**

© Pearson Education

Vowel Sound in *saw*

Spelling Words				
saw	draw	crawl	straw	law
jaw	paw	lawn	yawn	hawk

Draw lines through all the **p**'s and **o**'s.
Write the word that is left.

1. h o a p w p k o   1. _____

2. l o o a p w p n   2. _____

3. p c o r p a w p l   3. _____

4. y o a p w p p n o   4. _____

Write six list words that rhyme with **thaw**.

5. _____   6. _____

7. _____   8. _____

9. _____   10. _____

Home Activity Your child has been learning to spell words with the vowel sound in *saw*. Help your child use list words to make more word puzzles similar to those at the top of this page.

Spelling Practice Book

Prefixes *un-*, *re-*

Look at the word. **Say** it. **Listen** for the prefix.

Write the word.	**Check** it.

1. unhappy

2. refill

3. untie

4. undo

5. repay

6. unkind

7. undress

8. retell

9. reopen

10. refund

High-Frequency Words

11. different

12. carry

Home Activity Your child is learning to spell words with the prefixes *un-* and *re-*. To practice at home, have your child read the prefix, read the whole word, and spell the word.

School + Home

© Pearson Education

Prefixes *un-*, *re-*

Spelling Words				
unhappy	refill	untie	undo	repay
unkind	undress	retell	reopen	refund

Circle a word to finish the sentence. **Write** it.

_____

----

1. Will you   **unkind**   **untie**   my ribbon?   _____

----

2. She looks   **unhappy**   **repay**.   _____

----

3. Please   **refill**   **reopen**   the book.   _____

----

4. She will   **repay**   **unhappy**   you.   _____

----

5. Please   **retell**   **undress**   that story.   _____

----

6. I will   **retell**   **undress**   the doll.   _____

----

7. I got a   **refund**   **undo**   for the cap.   _____

----

8. Can you   **repay**   **undo**   this knot?   _____

----

9. He is   **refund**   **unkind**   to the dog.   _____

----

10. He will   **retell**   **refill**   the glasses.   _____

Home Activity Your child spelled words to complete sentences. Read a sentence on this page. Ask your child to identify the word with the prefix *re-* or *un-* and spell it.

© Pearson Education

Spelling Practice Book

Prefixes *un-*, *re-*

Spelling Words				
unhappy	refill	untie	undo	repay
unkind	undress	retell	reopen	refund

Write the prefix *un-* or *re-*. **Write** the list word.

_____   _____

1. Dad will _____ tell the joke.   _____

2. I can _____ tie my shoes.   _____

3. Let's _____ do this puzzle.   _____

4. He was _____ kind to Sam.   _____

5. She is _____ happy.   _____

6. You must _____ pay the loan.   _____

7. The men will _____ open the crate.   _____

8. I got a _____ fund for the tickets.   _____

9. Can you _____ fill my water bottle?   _____

10. I will _____ dress now.   _____

Home Activity Your child wrote words with the prefixes *un-* and *re-*. Have your child name the base word in each list word and tell how adding the prefix changes the meaning.

Prefixes *un-*, *re-*

Spelling Words				
unhappy	refill	untie	undo	repay
unkind	undress	retell	reopen	refund

Read the words in the box.
Add *un-* or *re-* to make a list word. **Write** it.

pay	tell
fund	fill

1. _____   2. _____

3. _____   4. _____

Find a list word in each row of letters. **Circle** it. **Write** it.

5. **r u n t i e s t**   5. _____

6. **t h r e o p e n**   6. _____

7. **u n k i n d e s**   7. _____

8. **x u n d r e s s**   8. _____

9. **w i u n d o t s**   9. _____

10. **s u n h a p p y**   10. _____

Home Activity Your child has been learning to spell words with the prefixes *un-* and *re-*. Help your child think of other words with these prefixes.

120 Unit 5 Week 6 **Day 4**

Spelling Practice Book

Short *a*

Unit 1, Week 1

1. at
2. can
3. cat
4. back
5. dad

6. am
7. bat
8. mad
9. ran
10. sack

Short *i* VC, CVC

Unit 1, Week 2

1. in
2. it
3. did
4. sit
5. six

6. fix
7. lip
8. mix
9. pin
10. wig

Short *o* CVC, CVCC

Unit 1, Week 3

1. mom
2. hot
3. hop
4. pot
5. pop

6. ox
7. lock
8. mop
9. got
10. rock

Adding -*s*

Unit 1, Week 4

1. nap
2. naps
3. sit
4. sits
5. win
6. wins

7. fit
8. fits
9. hit
10. hits

Short *e* CVC, CCVC

Unit 1, Week 5

1. bed
2. men
3. red
4. step
5. ten

6. net
7. leg
8. jet
9. sled
10. wet

Short *u* CVC, CVCC

Unit 1, Week 6

1. run
2. cut
3. must
4. sun
5. up

6. bump
7. jump
8. bus
9. nut
10. rug

Digraphs *sh*, *th*
Unit 2, Week 1

1. ship
2. fish
3. then
4. shut
5. with

6. rush
7. shell
8. shop
9. trash
10. thin

Long *a* CVCe
Unit 2, Week 2

1. face
2. made
3. age
4. safe
5. take

6. make
7. cage
8. cake
9. late
10. name

Long *i* CVCe
Unit 2, Week 3

1. like
2. ride
3. smile
4. time
5. white

6. bike
7. dime
8. hide
9. ice
10. kite

Long *o* CVCe
Unit 2, Week 4

1. home
2. hope
3. rose
4. woke
5. those

6. bone
7. hose
8. joke
9. rode
10. stone

Long *u* CVCe
Unit 2, Week 5

1. huge
2. June
3. rule
4. tube
5. use

6. cube
7. cute
8. flute
9. rude
10. mule

Long *e*: *e*, *ee*
Unit 2, Week 6

1. be
2. feet
3. he
4. see
5. we

6. green
7. me
8. she
9. tree
10. week

Digraphs ch, th Unit 2, Week 1	Long a CVCe Unit 2, Week 2	Long i CVCe Unit 2, Week 3
1. ship	1. whale	1. like
2. fish	2. made	2. ride
3. than	3. cage	3. smile
4. shut	4. safe	4. time
5. with	5. bake	5. white
6. trash	6. make	6. bike
7. shell	7. race	7. dime
8. shop	8. cake	8. nine
9. flash	9. late	9. ice
10. stiff	10. name	10. kite

Long o CVCe Unit 2, Week 4	Long u/VCe Unit 2, Week 5	Vowels e, ee Unit 2, Week 6
1. home	1. huge	1. be
2. rope	2. June	2. feel
3. rose	3. rule	3. he
4. woke	4. rope	4. see
5. those	5. use	5. we
6. bone	6. cube	6. green
7. hope	7. cute	7. me
8. joke	8. flute	8. she
9. vote	9. rude	9. tree
10. stone	10. mule	10. week

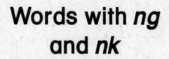

Long *e* and Long *i*: *y*
Unit 3, Week 1

1. my
2. by
3. try
4. any
5. body

6. fly
7. cry
8. lucky
9. silly
10. puppy

Words with *ng* and *nk*
Unit 3, Week 2

1. bring
2. trunk
3. pink
4. bank
5. sang

6. wing
7. rink
8. blank
9. rang
10. sunk

Adding -*es*
Unit 3, Week 3

1. fix
2. fixes
3. class
4. classes
5. wish
6. wishes

7. kiss
8. kisses
9. bus
10. buses

Adding -*ed*
Unit 3, Week 4

1. ask
2. asked
3. plan
4. planned
5. help
6. helped

7. jog
8. jogged
9. call
10. called

Words with *er*, *ir*, *ur*
Unit 3, Week 5

1. her
2. first
3. bird
4. girl
5. burn

6. were
7. shirt
8. fur
9. hurt
10. sir

Adding -*er* and -*est*
Unit 3, Week 6

1. bigger
2. biggest
3. faster
4. fastest
5. slower
6. slowest

7. shorter
8. shortest
9. sadder
10. saddest

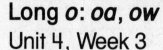

Long *a*: *ai, ay*
Unit 4, Week 1

1. train
2. way
3. tail
4. play
5. day

6. may
7. rain
8. gray
9. mail
10. afraid

Long *e*: *ea*
Unit 4, Week 2

1. eat
2. sea
3. each
4. team
5. please

6. dream
7. treat
8. beach
9. clean
10. lean

Long *o*: *oa, ow*
Unit 4, Week 3

1. boat
2. road
3. snow
4. row
5. yellow

6. loaf
7. coat
8. soap
9. blow
10. pillow

Long *i*: *ie, igh*
Unit 4, Week 4

1. lie
2. tie
3. high
4. might
5. right

6. night
7. bright
8. light
9. pie
10. tight

Compound Words
Unit 4, Week 5

1. backpack
2. outside
3. baseball
4. herself
5. flashlight

6. bluebird
7. lunchbox
8. suitcase
9. inside
10. brainstorm

Suffixes *-ly, -ful*
Unit 4, Week 6

1. slowly
2. careful
3. quickly
4. useful
5. painful

6. playful
7. sadly
8. gladly
9. nicely
10. wonderful

© Pearson Education

Vowel Sound in *how*
Unit 5, Week 1

1. how
2. town
3. down
4. now
5. brown

6. cow
7. clown
8. frown
9. crowd
10. growl

Vowel Sound in *out*
Unit 5, Week 2

1. mouth
2. house
3. found
4. our
5. out

6. cloud
7. ouch
8. shout
9. round
10. count

Vowel Sounds in *book* and *moon*
Unit 5, Week 3

1. book
2. moon
3. took
4. food
5. look

6. pool
7. zoo
8. noon
9. good
10. foot

Vowel Sound in *boy*
Unit 5, Week 4

1. oil
2. soil
3. voice
4. point
5. boy

6. boil
7. coin
8. oink
9. toy
10. join

Vowel Sound in *saw*
Unit 5, Week 5

1. saw
2. draw
3. crawl
4. straw
5. law

6. jaw
7. paw
8. lawn
9. yawn
10. hawk

Prefixes *un-*, *re-*
Unit 5, Week 6

1. unhappy
2. refill
3. untie
4. undo
5. repay

6. unkind
7. undress
8. retell
9. reopen
10. refund

© Pearson Education